Let's Explore a
RIVER

by Jane R. McCauley

Photographs by Joseph H. Bailey

A barred owl watches from a tree stump beside a river.

BOOKS FOR YOUNG EXPLORERS
NATIONAL GEOGRAPHIC SOCIETY

Caleb, Kelly, and Crystal are excited.
They are setting out with their father to explore
a river near their home. It is a sunny spring day.

Life vests protect the children in the canoe.
Their father helps Caleb tie his vest. Then off they go!

As the canoe drifts down the river, ripples move over the water. To the children, the river seems silent, as if nothing lived there. "Use your eyes and ears," their father whispers. "Things are hiding all around you."

The trees and plants along the river
are full of animals. Some stay out of sight
in the daytime. A bobcat may creep
down to the river to drink.

An egret flies low over the grasses
along the bank. The bird wades in shallow
water on its long legs and pokes
its long beak into the water to catch fish.
Close by, a rat snake climbs a tree.
Its muscles and its scaly skin
help keep the snake from slipping.

Kelly and Crystal dip their hands into the river and feel the water moving against their fingers. The movement of a river is called its current.

Plants growing on the river bottom move gently with the current. Large fish such as the Florida gar swim along the bottom, looking for smaller fish to eat.

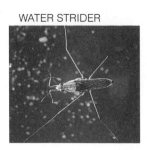
WATER STRIDER

SPIDER ON WATER LETTUCE

Caleb picks up a water lettuce plant to see what might be hiding there. A spider crawls over a leaf. An insect that lives on the surface of the river is the water strider. It can skate across the water.

A turtle is warming itself on a log. If it sees the family, the turtle might swiftly slide back into the river.

Near the river, the children wander among wild grapevines and cypress trees. A warbler sings from a branch. The "stumps" on the ground are parts of the roots of cypress trees. They are called knees.

ith a magnifying glass, Kelly looks closely at lichens on a branch. Lichens are plants that don't need soil to grow. Some kinds grow on rocks.

A fuzzy caterpillar tickles Crystal's fingers. Caleb carefully holds a tiny frog, but only for a few minutes. Many kinds of plants bloom in the woods in spring. Jack-in-the-pulpit grows in the shade. Violets add soft color.

FLORIDA VIOLETS

Thirsty and hungry, the family stops for a picnic.
After the busy morning, the food tastes good.
The children take off their shoes and rest for a while.

There are many enjoyable things to do along a river.
From her seat on a grapevine, Crystal watches
people paddling by in canoes.

On rubber tubes filled with air, people float lazily down the river with the current.

Some people ride rafts, and others swim. The river is so clear they can see the bottom.

Fishing from a pier can be fun. Crystal tries hard to catch a fish before her brother and sister do! She likes the way the water feels on her bare feet.

The children use pieces of bread as bait. A bird called a kingfisher doesn't need bait or a pole. It can dive off a branch and grab a fish from the river in its long beak.

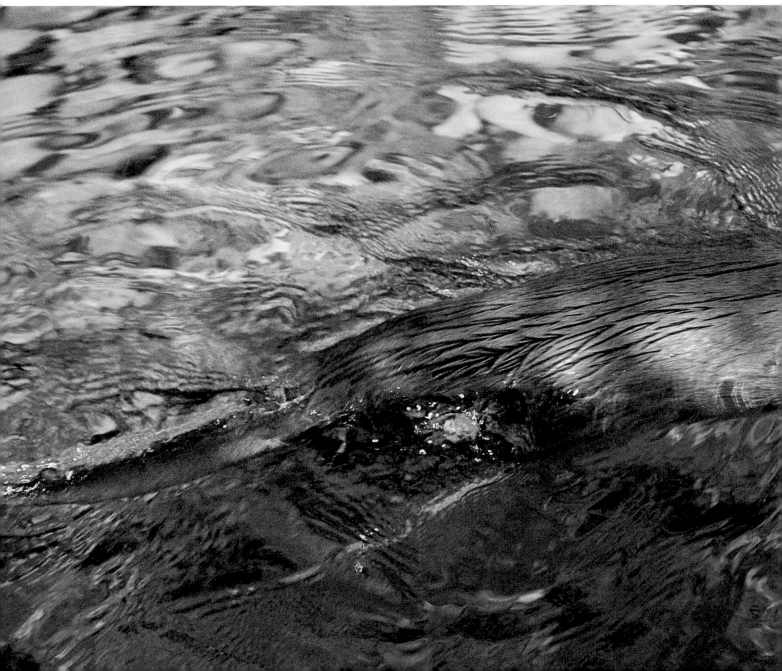

Otters are good at fishing, too. "Yummy," one seems to say, twitching its whiskers after a meal.

An otter glides through the water, paddling with its webbed feet. It steers with its furry tail. The otter pokes its whiskers and nose between the rocks and into the mud on the river bottom. It may find crayfish like this one to eat.

Time to cool off!
The children wade in shallow
water near the riverbank.
Their father watches
from the bank behind them.
The rocky bottom feels hard.
"Don't splash!" squeals Kelly.

A squirrel on a tree chatters as the canoe passes. Caleb has found more water lettuce. Kelly and Crystal break off one of the fungus plants growing on a dead tree. "It's like powder inside," Kelly says.

Near the end of their trip, the family paddles through a wide part of the river, where wild rice grows. The children will return another day. On their next visit, the river may look very different.

As the seasons change, the river changes, too.
On a winter day, a great blue heron walks
among the grasses by the river. It lives here all year.
So do many other creatures.

Few leaves cover the trees in winter.
The river seems empty. But Crystal, Kelly, and Caleb
have learned that something is happening all the time.

Published by
The National Geographic Society, Washington, D.C.
Gilbert M. Grosvenor, *President and Chairman of the Board*
Melvin M. Payne, Thomas W. McKnew, *Chairmen Emeritus*
Owen R. Anderson, *Executive Vice President*
Robert L. Breeden, *Senior Vice President,*
   Publications and Educational Media

Prepared by
The Special Publications and School Services Division
Donald J. Crump, *Director*
Philip B. Silcott, *Associate Director*
Bonnie S. Lawrence, *Assistant Director*

Staff for this book
Jane H. Buxton, *Managing Editor*
Karen G. Yee, *Illustrations Editor*
Cinda Rose, *Art Director*
Alice Jablonsky, *Researcher*
Artemis S. Lampathakis, *Illustrations Assistant*
Susan A. Bender, Marisa J. Farabelli, Sandra F. Lotterman,
   Eliza C. Morton, Dru McLoud Stancampiano, *Staff Assistants*

Engraving, Printing, and Product Manufacture
George V. White, *Director,*
   Manufacturing and Quality Management
Vincent P. Ryan, *Manager,*
   Manufacturing and Quality Management
David V. Showers, *Production Manager*
Kathleen M. Cirucci, *Production Project Manager*
Carol R. Curtis, *Senior Production Staff Assistant*

Consultants
Richard Franz, Florida Museum of Natural History;
   Dr. Walter Judd, Department of Botany, University of Florida;
   Craig Parenteau, Biologist, Florida Park Service,
   Scientific Consultants
Susan W. Altemus, *Educational Consultant*
Dr. Lynda Bush, *Reading Consultant*

Illustrations Credits
All photographs by National Geographic Photographer Joseph H. Bailey
except: Jen and Des Bartlett (1); ANIMALS ANIMALS/Ted Levin (6);
© 1988 Doug Perrine (9 lower); James H. Robinson (10 right); Karen G.
Yee/N.G.S. Staff (10 lower); C. C. Lockwood (12 upper); Bob and Clara
Calhoun/Bruce Coleman Inc. (20 upper); L. L. Rue III/Bruce Coleman
Inc. (22 upper); Stephen J. Krasemann/The National Audubon Society
Collection/PR (22-23); Wes C. Skiles (23 upper).

The Society gratefully acknowledges the cooperation of Azell Nail and his
family; the staff at Ichetucknee Springs State Park, Fort White, Florida;
Mary Ann Twyford, Florida Department of Natural Resources; and The
Great Outdoors Trading Company, High Springs, Florida.

Library of Congress CIP Data
McCauley, Jane R.
   Let's explore a river.
   (Books for young explorers)
   Bibliography: p.
   Summary: Three children accompany their father in a canoe and explore the plant
and animal life along a river near their home.
   1. Stream ecology—Juvenile literature.   2. Rivers—Juvenile literature.
[1. Stream animals.   2. Stream plants.   3. Rivers]   I. Bailey, Joseph H.,
ill.   II. Title: River.   III. Series.
QH541.5.S7M39   1988   508.316'93   88-25349
   ISBN   0-87044-741-6 (regular edition)
   ISBN   0-87044-746-7 (library edition)

"Look at me. I'm a monkey," Caleb says, as he
swings on a grapevine. Caleb discovered many
plants and animals by the river.

COVER: Stretched out on a dock, Caleb peers down
into the water with a waterscope made from a milk
carton. He can see tiny plants and animals that drift
below the water's surface. Follow the directions
in *More About* to make your own waterscope to
take along when you explore a river.

MORE ABOUT

A heron stands motionless along the banks. Ducks take flight from the grasses. Sunlight dapples the water, where swarms of insects buzz and hum. A river's natural beauty can provide you and your children hours of pleasure on a summer afternoon or on a crisp fall day, even on a frosty winter morning. Rivers vary with the seasons, during storms, and as they flow past hills and valleys, under bridges and highways. There is always something new to notice each time you visit.

By canoe and on foot, park manager Azell Nail and his children—Crystal, age 9, Kelly, 7, and Caleb, 5—explored northern Florida's Ichetucknee River. For half of its six-mile course, the river winds through woods and swamps in the Ichetucknee Springs State Park. Unlike many rivers, which begin as mountain streams, the Ichetucknee derives from a series of underground springs; its water remains crystal clear and a constant 72°F to 73°F—ideal for activities such as snorkeling. Underwater limestone caves attract divers. Slow-moving in many places, the river ranges from three to twelve feet in depth.

Like most rivers, the Ichetucknee offers sanctuary to a diversity of plants and animals. Barred owls (1),* tree frogs (14), woodpeckers, and rat snakes (7) inhabit trees and bushes beside the water. At night a bobcat (6) may venture out. Many creatures depend on the river for food or drink.

The food chain of the river is aided by the current, which sweeps nutrients to fish, crustaceans, plants, and other living things. Current is the direction and speed of water movement. It changes along a river's course and at different depths. The current varies during the day and in different seasons. To help explain currents to your children, have them feel the movement of the water with their hands, just as Kelly and Crystal did (8-9).

Some animals, such as the crayfish, dwell on the river bottom. This lobster relative is most active at night. Be wary of picking up a crayfish; it has claws that can pinch sharply.

Among the mammals that find food in rivers are otters (22-23). They

What hides beneath the surface of the water? To find out, Kelly and Caleb make waterscopes from milk cartons. Through the waterscopes, they can see plants, rocks, and tiny spots that look like dirt. These flecks may fool them. They may be animals!

*Numbers in parentheses refer to pages in *Let's Explore a River.*

probe for crayfish in underwater nooks with their nimble front feet and muzzles. Otters are shy, elusive creatures that seem to play hide-and-seek. One will surface, dive again, then moments later appear on the opposite shore.

In woodlands beside the Ichetucknee, thick grapevines loop through tall cypress trees (12-13). Knees that grow from the cypress roots may help stabilize the trees in thin soil, or they may help the roots breathe when the roots are submerged in water.

Crystal, Kelly, and Caleb found lichens (15) on rocks and branches. Lichens are actually made of two plants—an alga and a fungus. They have no roots, stems, or leaves. Yet these hardy plants anchor easily on rocks, stone, and wood. The children saw shelf fungi (27) growing on dead trees. Shelf fungi are saprophytes, plants that live off decaying matter; they lack the chlorophyll necessary to manufacture their own food. Examining lichens, fungi, and wildflowers through a simple magnifying glass can make learning about them fun for your child.

A popular pastime on the Ichetucknee River is tubing (18-19). Since tubing and other recreational activities can damage the river's fragile plant life, park officials limit the number of people allowed to use the river at one time. Tubers are encouraged not to hold onto the vegetation and to stay within certain areas. It is important to help your children be thoughtful explorers by leaving the plants and wildlife for others to enjoy.

Following Crystal, Kelly, and Caleb on their river journey can give you ideas for ways to investigate other rivers with your children. For most boating activities, all participants should wear life jackets, especially on fast-flowing rivers with rapids.

When you visit a river, look for the tiny creatures and plants beneath the water's surface. You do not need a canoe or other boat. You can construct an inexpensive waterscope to view underwater life, as the Nail children did. Here's how you can help your child make one:

• Gather a half-gallon milk carton, scissors, tape (freezer tape works best), and thick plastic (kitchen plastic will work, but a thicker type such as that used for weatherstripping is better).

• Cut off the top and the bottom of the milk carton. Then tape the bottom edge of the carton so it will not tear the plastic.

• Cover the bottom and sides with the plastic, taping it to the outside. Hold the plastic in place with a rubber band while you tape it.

Your waterscope is now finished! Place the plastic-covered end of it in the water. Make sure you tilt the waterscope as you do this to keep air from being trapped between the plastic and the water. And be careful not to get water in the open end! You may find that your waterscope works better on a cloudy day or when your shadow falls on it. Some places in the water are busier than others, so move around until you find some action. You will see a small world of living things that make the river their home.

ADDITIONAL READING

America's Wild and Scenic Rivers. (Wash., D.C., National Geographic Society, 1983). Family reading.

Rivers and Lakes, by Peter Credland. (Danbury, Conn., Danbury Press, 1975). Ages 10 and up.

Still Waters, White Waters, by Ron Fisher. (Wash., D.C., National Geographic Society, 1977). Family reading.

This Is a River, by Laurence Pringle. (N.Y., MacMillan Company, 1972). Ages 6 and up.

The World of the Otter, by Ed Park. (Philadelphia, J. B. Lippincott Company, 1971). Ages 10 and up.

"Leaves of three, let them be." Remembering this saying when you explore in wooded areas can help you avoid poison ivy. This plant, which grows on trees and on the ground, can cause an itchy rash if you touch it.